NML/NFK90

D0319222

WITHDRAWN
FROM STOCK

WITHDRAWN
FROM STOCK

NORFOLK

A portrait in colour

ROBERT HALLMANN & KEITH SKIPPER

COUNTRYSIDE BOOKS

Other counties in this series include:

BUCKINGHAMSHIRE	LINCOLNSHIRE
CHESHIRE	NOTTINGHAMSHIRE
DERBYSHIRE	SHROPSHIRE
DEVON	SUFFOLK
ESSEX	SURREY
LEICESTERSHIRE & RUTLAND	SUSSEX
LANCASHIRE	WARWICKSHIRE

First published 2002
© Text, Keith Skipper 2002
© Photographs, Robert Hallmann 2002

All rights reserved.
No reproduction permitted
without the prior permission
of the publisher:

COUNTRYSIDE BOOKS
3 Catherine Road
Newbury, Berkshire

To view our complete range of books,
please visit us at
www.countrysidebooks.co.uk

ISBN 1 85306 693 1

The photograph on page 1 is of Brancaster and
that on page 4 is of Walsingham Abbey

Designed by Mon Mohan
Produced through MRM Associates Ltd., Reading
Printed in Italy

L942.61

NORFOLK LIBRARY AND
INFORMATION SERVICE

SUPP	JARROLD
INV.NO.	116551
ORD DATE	22.10.02

Contents

INTRODUCTION

'If the rest of Britain sank beneath the waves, and Norfolk was left alone, islanded in the turmoil of the seas, it would, I think, survive without too much trouble... Norfolk has always stood alone and aloof from the rest of England.'
James Wentworth Day (1976)

Norfolk is the most faithful of old friends. While others may be tempted to flirt with passing fancies, Norfolk stays steadfastly true to those who care about distinctiveness and the desire to be different.

I have relished such a friendship and its associated values ever since I realised it was my inestimable good fortune to be born and raised in a county of infinite variety with a spirit of independence that has been squeezed dry in so many other places.

Norfolk continues to tell me that more does not mean better. Norfolk reminds me constantly not to confuse change with invariable progress. Norfolk welcomes visitors and newcomers with an admonishing finger pointing to the fate of counties from which most are pleased to escape.

In short, this is a special part of the country with a pride and self-confidence born out of comparative isolation and a firm belief that there is nothing wrong with protecting your own instincts and interests.

It has been a source of deep satisfaction to help produce this portrait of Norfolk. I found reassurance in the familiar ... and then watched in wonder as Robert Hallmann applied fresh coats of paint. His pictures do justice to all we hold dear under Norfolk's vast skies, from the grandest country house to cricket on the village green. Just as significantly, they have the power to encourage even the most passionate of natives not to take old friends for granted.

I was born and brought up in a small mid-Norfolk village and went to grammar school in Swaffham. I worked in Thetford, Dereham, Yarmouth and Norwich on newspapers and local radio. I live now with my family on the North Norfolk coast, ruminating, writing and counting my blessings. When people say I haven't moved far over the years, I smile and tell them there's simply been no need.

Old friends must be cherished.

Keith Skipper

Diss

'Dear Mary, yes, it will be bliss
To go with you by train to Diss,
Your walking shoes upon your feet,
We'll meet, my sweet, at Liverpool Street.'

John Betjeman (1906-1984) *A Mind's Journey to Diss*

Poet Laureate Sir John Betjeman voted Diss his favourite Norfolk town. One of his poems recalls a train trip to Diss with Mary Wilson, wife of Sir Harold Wilson, our Prime Minister in the 1960s.

Lady Wilson lived here as a child and retained strong affection for an attractive town built around a six-acre mere, or lake, and boasting a fine collection of half-timbered houses, some with carved corner posts and others with bold plaster pargeting. Fears that electrification of the railway line to London would reduce Diss to a bland chunk of commuterland have happily proved largely unfounded.

Local history comes alive on the town sign, one of many in the county carved by Harry Carter, my old art and handicrafts master at Hamond's Grammar School in Swaffham. On one side are featured a couple in medieval costume: 'Matilda, daughter of Walter Fitz Walter (the Valiant), Lord of the Manor of Diss, rejected the advances of King John. The angry king sent a messenger with a poisoned Potched egg – whereof she died, 1213.' This fatal snack provided only a taste of John's despicable behaviour during a long reign.

On the other side, the man reckoned to be our first Poet Laureate is seen giving instruction to Henry VII's children, the Princesses Margaret and Mary and the young Prince Henry, later King Henry VIII. John Skelton was rector at the parish church of St Mary the Virgin for 25 years from 1504 until his death in 1529.

A fine scholar, Skelton was also a scurrilous and vituperative rebel. He used his poetry to attack enemies, and his work was highly original and notable for use of the vernacular in short lines. He loved to shock. On one occasion he stood in the pulpit and held up a love-child, fathered by himself, to show the congregation, daring anyone to find fault with it or himself.

Billingford Mill

'On a small green platform crowning a field of waving barley stands the windmill seen for miles around, the most picturesque feature on this sunny landscape, and to our delight is seen whirling round in its old-fashioned way, careless of the counter advantages of machinery and steam.'

Clement Scott (1841–1904) *Poppy-Land*

There are two villages in Norfolk called Billingford – and the other one, near East Dereham, has a water mill. This Billingford, a couple of miles east of Diss, is noted for having the last Norfolk corn mill to work by wind. It was in operation until 1956.

This landmark building on Billingford Common then became the first corn mill to be acquired for preservation by the Norfolk Windmills Trust in 1965. It is regularly open to visitors and the old post office in the village sells bread baked by a local baker from flour ground at the mill. A tasty link with the past.

A five-storey brick tower mill with a Norfolk boat-shaped cap and six-bladed fantail, it has most of its original machinery and equipment intact. Built between 1859 and 1860 at a cost of £1,300, the present tower replaced a post mill on the site blown down in September 1859. An account of that disaster in the *Norfolk News* included details of a dramatic escape as the building was reduced to a heap of ruins in a few seconds:

'Two persons were inside the mill at the time, George Goddard the occupier and an old man in his employ. The latter was seriously hurt, but Goddard's escape was almost miraculous. He was at the top of the mill at the time of its going over and was precipitated to a depth of five and twenty feet, along with the mass of falling rubbish and when found was standing wedged in between the mill stones and a large cog wheel close by – the whole weighing nearly three tons.'

Long Stratton (*inset*), straddling the busy A140 road from Norwich to Ipswich, is one of the fastest-growing communities in the county, but still takes pride in a number of timber-framed houses round the centre and pleasant old-fashioned houses and villas towards the south. St Mary's church has a round tower and is home to a sexton's wheel, of which there is only one other known example – at Yaxley in Suffolk. It is a sort of revolving calendar indicating festivals and fasts.

Wymondham

'In reparation and honour to a noble and courageous leader in the struggles of the common people of England to escape from a servile life to the freedom of present conditions.'
Plaque to Wymondham's Robert Kett at the entrance to Norwich Castle, placed there four centuries after the doomed rebellion he led in 1549.

This busy town with an obvious feel for its own history provides one of Norfolk's favourite pronunciation pot-holes. Newcomers and visitors trip up regularly to give chuckling locals a chance to tell them it is pronounced 'Windham' – just one example of how the county delights in doing things differently.

Wymondham has more listed buildings than any similar-sized town in Norfolk, most of them built after the disastrous fire of 1615. The octagonal Market Cross (*opposite*) went up to replace what was probably a Tudor market hall destroyed in the blaze. Townsfolk conducted their business around it, and the Market Court, which ensured that rules governing the Friday market were observed, held its meeting at the Cross. With the advent of the railway, the market declined and the Cross was used as a subscription library from about 1870 until 1912.

Wymondham's most celebrated son was a tanner and landowner who led the Norfolk peasantry against enclosure of common land by the gentry. Robert Kett was an outstanding champion, but the rebellion of 1549 ended, inevitably, in defeat. He was found guilty of treason and hanged at Norwich Castle. His brother William was hanged from the tower of Wymondham Abbey.

Four miles west of Wymondham, the small town of Hingham (*inset*) comes as a grand surprise, with Jane Austen-style houses surrounding the Market Place. A number of Hingham people embarked on a new life in America in the early 17th century. They founded the colony of Bare Cove, now renamed Hingham, in Massachusetts. In 1637 they were joined by local boy Samuel Lincoln, great-great-great-great-grandfather of Abraham Lincoln. Ties between the two Hinghams remain strong, and St Andrew's church contains a memorial to the Lincoln family.

The Buckenhams

'Of this world's goods he had his share,
Both wine and punch as well as beer
His whole life thro' he did not spare'
Inscription on tomb of John Hill (died 1765) near the door of St Martin's church, New Buckenham.

The Buckenhams make a handsome pair in the South Norfolk countryside even though they are so different in shape and character.

Old Buckenham surrounds a vast village green with clusters of houses and lanes carrying intriguing names like Hog's Snout and Puddledock. Ponds on the fringe of the green probably represent old clay and gravel quarries. By contrast, New Buckenham is a carefully planned settlement, England's best example of a Norman new town.

After the Conquest, the manor was given to William d'Albini, one of William the Conqueror's main supporters, who built a castle at Old Buckenham. This has gone. His son, also named William, created New Buckenham in 1146, building a new castle with the first round keep in the country and laying out beside it a grid of streets, two hundred yards square, and a broad market place surrounded by a bank ditch.

All this survives, including the tiny chapel of St Mary, the town's first church, now incorporated into a barn to the east of the castle. Many cottages are thatched and timber-framed, and standing on the green, the former market place, is the 1559 Court House, raised on Tuscan columns. The middle column served as a whipping post and still has its manacles of iron.

The new church of St Martin (*opposite*) was built in 1254 and rebuilt by Sir John Knyvett in 1479 when the whole of the exterior was decorated with flint flushwork and the new roof was given its corbels representing the Apostles.

An extension to the village hall at Old Buckenham reflects more recent history. The 453rd Bomb Group Memorial Room was opened by film star James Stewart in 1983. From March 1944 the Hollywood legend was the Group's Operations Officer, and while he was there one of the Group's squadrons, the 733rd, set an unbeaten record of 82 missions without loss. What remains of the old airfield lies to the north-east of the village.

Norwich Cathedral

'Norwich the incomparable city, which all must know who would England know... the Cathedral has a lovely spire which might well have tempted Constable and saved him the journey down to Salisbury.'

Arthur Mee (1873-1943) *The King's England*

One of the great Norman buildings of England, its spire dominating the city like a giant finger beckoning all to view this exquisite structure, Norwich Cathedral was begun by Bishop Herbert de Losinga in 1096.

His 'Church of Norwich' was consecrated in 1101 although it was not to be completed for many years. By the time Bishop Herbert died in 1119 it was built as far as the twisted pillars. His body was laid before the high altar in a splendid tomb. Both this tomb and its 18th-century successor have gone. Now a black marble slab set in the floor before the high altar marks his grave, around which six iron candlesticks linked with white rope stand guard – a fitting monument to the man who wrote of his church and the Benedictine monastery he built to serve it: 'Remember, you enjoy this advantage at my expense, whose toils and labours have won it for you.'

Later bishops replaced the original timber roofs and spire and added windows in the Gothic style. Just a few points of distinction are the Anglo-Saxon consecration stones below the Bishop's Throne; the ancient design of the apse with a walkway round the high chancel and radiating chapels; the 700 carved roof bosses and the carved misericords telling stories from Christian mythology and history, and also depicting everyday life in medieval and Tudor times. The medieval painted reredos in St Luke's Chapel is another of the countless treasures.

The Cathedral stands in a beautiful close which retains much of its old atmosphere despite the encroachment of the car and conversion into offices of many stately 18th-century houses. In the Upper Close, the 14th-century grammar school is overlooked by a figure of former pupil Horatio Nelson.

Norwich – A Fine Old City

*'A fine old city truly is that, view it from whatever side you will; but it shows best from the east,
where the ground, bold and elevated, overlooks the fair and fertile valley in which it stands.'*

George Borrow (1803-1881) *Lavengro*

Perhaps the most famous tribute to Norwich came from gypsy champion George Borrow. His epithet 'A fine old city', first aired in his novel *Lavengro* in 1851, has been used liberally on signs greeting visitors and in many other areas of publicity. Borrow was standing on Mousehold Heath on the edge of the city when he did the advertising business such a big favour.

In fact, Borrow was echoing praise heaped on the place by earlier illustrious figures. Sir John Harington said in 1612: 'I should judge this city to be another Utopia.' Thomas Fuller waxed lyrical in 1662: 'It is either a city in an orchard, or an orchard in a city'. When diarist John Evelyn paid a call in 1671 he described it as: 'One of the largest, and certainly, after London, one of the noblest in England.' William Cobbett included Norfolk on his famous *Rural Rides* in the 1820s, and on visiting Norwich to attend the Radical Reform Dinner he pronounced: 'The meat and poultry and vegetable market is beautiful.'

Most visitors today make sure to take in Elm Hill (*opposite*), the city's tourist showpiece. This narrow, cobbled street full of delightful old buildings has the air of a film set – but it is as real as flint and seasoned oak. Half a century ago it was threatened with wholesale demolition. Salvation came largely through the efforts of the Norwich Society, founded especially for the purpose.

Cow Tower (*inset*), one of the most intriguing landmarks on a riverside walk, part of an eight-mile pathway beside the Wensum, got its name as grazing beasts rubbed themselves against it and sheltered by it. But the tower's original role was far more businesslike. It was the toll house from which the servants of the Prior of Norwich collected payment from vessels plying the river between city and coast.

Great Yarmouth

'Peggotty said, with greater emphasis than usual, that we must take things as we found them, and that, for her part, she was proud to call herself a Yarmouth Bloater.'
Charles Dickens (1812-1870) *David Copperfield*

A national playground to many, with its neon lights, amusement arcades, caravan sites, funfairs and inviting sands, Yarmouth is also a market town, working port — and home to a remarkable amount of fascinating history.

It has one of the most complete medieval town walls in England, the biggest parish church in the country (largely rebuilt after falling victim to the Luftwaffe in 1942), a unique grid-iron formation of narrow lanes known as The Rows, impressive ancient buildings galore and proud literary links with the likes of Charles Dickens, Anna Sewell and Daniel Defoe. Add the Nelson touch, and you have some measure of the importance of the place beyond its reputation as a popular family resort.

Norfolk's favourite son, born at Burnham Thorpe in 1758, was close to Yarmouth and its people. Lord Nelson stepped ashore here after the Battle of the Nile and was accorded a tumultuous reception. More wild rejoicing greeted him following the great victory at Copenhagen. After his death at Trafalgar, the Nelson Monument (*inset*) was erected through public subscription on the South Denes in his honour. In fact, Britannia stands in triumph at the top holding a trident and laurel wreath and looking towards the naval hero's birthplace.

The port was revitalised after the decline of the fishing industry by the discovery of oil and gas in the North Sea. Some say the Golden Mile and all its associated holiday attractions will need a dramatic overhaul if Yarmouth is to stay in step with latest demands in the pleasure-seeking market. Big changes are planned, but it would be folly to surrender completely that brash and breezy kiss-me-quick formula favoured by so many generations.

As Peggotty said to wide-eyed young Copperfield, we must take things as we find them rather than strive to be like everyone else.

18

Broadland

'There is no better playground in England – and certainly none easier of access or more cheaply to be enjoyed'
George Christopher Davies, 'The Man Who Found The Broads', (1849-1922) *Norfolk Broads and Rivers*, 1883

Broadland pioneers of the Victorian age simply could not have foreseen the way this network of meandering rivers and expanses of open water would prove so popular ... causing ripples of controversy.

Conservation measures have been progressively introduced and reserves created, but there was little to protect the Broads from the post-war consequences of the growth of population, the revolution in farming methods and the boom in the yachting and motor boat industry. Precious flora and fauna were gravely damaged, but bold steps have been taken and institutions set up to introduce a measure of overall control. In 1988 status was given to the Broads comparable to that of a National Park, and the great battle between a buoyant economy and a fragile ecology now appears to be more evenly balanced.

The Broads were created in the Middle Ages when rising sea levels flooded ancient peat workings, forming a series of lakes interlaced with dykes and rivers. The principal rivers – the Yare, the Waveney and the Bure, with its tributaries the Thurne and the Ant – together provide nearly 200 miles of navigable waterways. The windmill has decorated the landscape since medieval times and was used both to grind corn and as a drainage pump.

The white-faced windpump at busy Thurne Dyke (*opposite*) is one of the most distinctive Broadland mills, and is known locally as 'Jack'. The sister mill, 'Jenny', is across the water, and when the wind is strong the two may be seen turning together.

When the holiday haunts become too hectic for comfort, there are peaceful refuges on hand. The Fairhaven Gardens Trust in the Broadland village of South Walsham has attractive walks with picturesque bridges over water gardens. Primulas and rhododendrons are seasonal specialities, while the historic King Oak (*inset*) is a constant attraction. It is over 900 years old – and home to many owls who like a tranquil setting.

Horsey

'When the sea comes in at Horsey Gap
Without any previous warning,
A swan shall build its rushy nest
On the roof of the Swan at Horning.
And a bald-headed crow, contented and merry
Shall feast on the corpses that float by the ferry.'

Anon

That ancient rhyme conjures up grisly images in one of Norfolk's most atmospheric corners where the land is flat and exposed. Victorian novelist Wilkie Collins used Horsey Mere as one of the compelling backcloths for his novel *Armadale*, published in 1866: 'The world and the world's turmoil seemed left behind forever on the land. The silence was the silence of enchantment – the delicious interflow of the soft purity of the sky and the bright tranquillity of the lake.'

A vastly different story unfolded on 13th February 1938, when the seas were whipped into a frenzy by a northerly gale which left a trail of destruction from The Wash to Southwold. The small community of Horsey, a mile from the coast and seven miles north of Yarmouth, bore the brunt of this invasion. Bursting over the low-lying coastline between Winterton and Palling, a tidal wave made the biggest breach for 50 years and flooded 15 square miles of farms and marshes. Houses were surrounded by the sea and occupants had to be evacuated. Many knew nothing of the oncoming waves until they found them within a few yards of their homes.

Horsey Mere is part of a Site of Special Scientific Interest on 2,000 acres of marshland, marrams and farmland. Many rare birds can be spotted here, including the marsh harrier, osprey, black tern and bittern. Horsey Windpump (*inset*) stands imperiously alongside the dyke leading to the Mere, where there is a private staithe. There are grand views across the marshes from this four-storey windpump, which was acquired by the National Trust in 1948 and subsequently restored. It is open during daylight hours in the summer.

Potter Heigham

'Blessed are they that live near Potter Heigham – and double blessed are they that live in it!'

Old Norfolk saw

Perhaps that rather flattering tribute to one of Broadland's main boating centres owes something to having Sidney Grapes, the much-loved Norfolk comedian, as a resident all his life. Son of a local builder and carpenter, he opened a bicycle shop which grew into a garage as traffic increased and the village developed into a bustling holiday magnet.

Just after the last war he was inspired to write to the main local paper, the *Eastern Daily Press*, the first of a series of letters written in Norfolk dialect and signed 'The Boy John'. He kept up the supply on an occasional basis until his death in 1958, assuming the character of a rustic who wrote as he spoke and spelled as he pleased. The Boy John Letters, drawn from the heart of village life, were circulated and enjoyed all over the world wherever East Anglians had settled.

Potter Heigham became known as The Boy John's village and some still call it such today out of undimmed affection for an endearing personality who was a keen servant of the parish church. St Nicholas', with its pretty thatch, stands out in the village proper well away from the tourist bustle.

The narrow hump-backed bridge whose three low stone arches span the River Thurne is well over 600 years old. Since 1969, when a new bypass was built along the line of the old Midland and Great Northern Railway, Potter Heigham bridge has ceased to be the bane of motor traffic, simply carrying the lesser volume of the village itself. While it is admired by artists and historians, helmsmen approach it with trepidation. It's been the ruin of much paintwork and many canopies and windscreens. On the other hand, those who like a quieter scene claim that the old bridge serves a useful purpose in limiting holiday traffic up the Thurne to the nature reserves of Hickling Broad and Horsey Mere.

Sea Palling and Happisburgh

'Here churches were gaunt fortresses against gales; they reared exposed from the last salt-bitten acres. Parish after parish, the flint church towers stood four-square, indomitably upright, guardians of the land, watchers of the sea.'

William Riviere, *Watercolour Sky,* 1990

Drop in on Sea Palling (*opposite*) any bright day and you'll find the ideal haunt of people seeking spacious and unspoilt beaches. When the village first became a holiday retreat early in the 20th century its name – once spelt Pawling or Pauling – rapidly acquired the prefix 'Sea'. A justifiable addition for the North Sea had long shaped the course of Palling's history, providing a living for most of the population while remorselessly encroaching on their property and land.

Drop in as the summer sun shines and villagers look up from their gardens to exchange pleasantries. A hybrid place, soil next to sandhills and surf, flowers nodding towards the foam and caravans surrounding homes where people live all the time. They have felt the full anger of the North Sea round here, not least with the tidal surge of 1953 which led to the building of a continuous sea wall from Eccles to Winterton. The sea, seemingly determined to put paid to Palling over the centuries, was instrumental in saving it ...

In 1968, Norfolk County Council planners supported new seaside 'towns' to be built at Hemsby and Sea Palling. Six years later, a planning application to site one such development at Palling looked cut and dried as a public inquiry opened at the village hall. Then the £8 million project faded away following evidence from the chief assistant engineer of the East Suffolk and Norfolk Rivers Authority. When asked if another tidal surge could breach defences, he said it was a small risk – but it could happen. Seaside 'overspill' plans were dropped. Sea Palling has been left alone to look after its simple Norfolk soul.

Along the coast towards Cromer, the skyline around Happisburgh (delightfully pronounced Hazeburrer) is ringed by tall landmarks ... several church towers, water towers, radio masts, pylons, the gas terminal at Bacton, the candy-stripe lighthouse (*inset*) built in 1791 and the soaring spire of St Mary's church.

Full Steam Ahead!

'Dick and Dorothea Callum had never been in Norfolk before and for ten minutes they had been waiting in
(Thorpe) station, sitting in the train for fear it should go again at once as it had at Ipswich...'

Arthur Ransome (1884-1967), *Coot Club*, 1934

It is one of the ironies of this high-speed age that many people who normally resist the charms of public transport take to it with relish when they are on holiday. And a nostalgic trip back to the golden age of steam is not to be missed ... Norfolk provides perfect platforms for growing numbers of such time travellers.

The old Midland and Great Northern line (known affectionately as the Muddle and Get Nowhere) ran from Cromer to Sheringham, Weybourne, Holt and Melton Constable from 1887, but by 1964 all except the Cromer to Sheringham section had fallen foul of Dr Beeching's notorious axe. A preservation society was set up and the line has been reopened with steam trains chugging through some of the prettiest scenery in the county. North Norfolk Railway's Poppy Line is mainly run by volunteers. Much has been achieved since they took over from British Rail, with Sheringham station (*opposite*) partly converted into a museum. Locomotives and rolling stock, railway bygones, a signal box and a model railway are on show along with a W H Smith bookstall on long-term loan from the National Railway Museum, having stood for many years on the concourse of London's Waterloo station.

The Bure Valley Railway (*inset*), a 15-inch gauge affair built in 1990 and mainly operated by steam locomotives, runs for nine attractive miles between Aylsham and Hoveton and Wroxham, 'Capital of the Broads'. There are stops in the charming villages of Brampton, Buxton and Coltishall.

National Trust Jewels

'The first sight of Blickling Hall is one of the greatest surprises that can possibly befall the traveller in search of the picturesque.'
Charles Harper, *The Newmarket, Bury, Thetford and Cromer Road*, 1904

The last great house to be built in Norfolk in the Jacobean style, Blickling Hall, just over a mile west of Aylsham, is one of the area's most spectacular attractions (*opposite*). The 17th-century red-brick house is flanked by two immense yew hedges, has an extensive garden and is surrounded by wonderful parkland and woodland. It looks a treat ... and lives up to expectations.

Most principal rooms are open to the public, including the Long Gallery with its outstanding library, the Chinese Bedroom with hand-painted wallpaper and the Peter the Great Room, dominated by its massive tapestry of the Russian Tsar at the Battle of Pottawa. Anne Boleyn, second queen of Henry VIII, may have lived at Blickling as a girl – and there are plenty of fanciful tales to go with that tasty historic titbit!

The gardens have remarkable herbaceous borders, each based on one colour, and the walk to the Tuscan temple is a blaze of colour in early summer when rhododendrons and azaleas are in full bloom. The 'secret garden' was much loved by the 11th Marquis of Lothian, who gave the estate to the National Trust in 1940. There is also an 18th-century orangery ... and a mausoleum shaped like a pyramid in the park. It contains the remains of John Hobart, 2nd Earl of Buckinghamshire, and his family.

Felbrigg Hall (*inset*), a few miles away near Cromer, was left to the National Trust in 1969 by outstanding Norfolk scholar Robert Ketton-Cremer. Built for Thomas Windham around 1620 and enlarged in subsequent centuries, the house has an outstanding library and collection of pictures. In the charming grounds is an orangery and in the walled gardens, a restored dovecote and herb garden.

For many, the full beauty of the Felbrigg environment is best appreciated with a good walk, taking in the isolated village church in the park, the Great Wood and the ornamental lake merged from a group of ponds in the 1750s.

Cromer

'You should have gone to Cromer, my dear, if you went anywhere – Perry was a week at Cromer once, and he holds it to be the best of all the sea-bathing places. A fine open sea, he says, and very pure air.'

Jane Austen (1775–1817) *Emma*, 1816

Perry's seaside sentiments could be taken down, dusted and used in evidence nearly two centuries later. Cromer never goes out of fashion because it pays no heed to trends or slick tricks of the holiday trade.

Yes, I'm slightly biased, having made the Gem of the Norfolk Coast my family home in 1988, but even its harshest critics accept that the place has reviving powers built on fresh air and tradition. Nowhere are these more pronounced than on the pier, which celebrated its

centenary in 2001. It is a haven for those who relish the old Norfolk trick of having one foot on land and the other in the sea. There's room to think and to enjoy the scenery, especially the town tumbling towards you if the church lets go.

At the seaward end stands the Pavilion Theatre, with the last authentic end-of-the-pier summer show in the country, and the new lifeboat house behind it. The prospect of serious action down the slipway adds drama to any performance on stage when the winds blow and seas are choppy. The pier was sliced in half by a runaway barge in November 1993, and became one of the county's leading tourist 'attractions' before a new holiday season beckoned with the official reopening six months later.

A bronze bust of Cromer's most famous son looks down on the waves from North Lodge Park. Henry Blogg (*inset*) was lifeboat coxswain for 38 years, with 53 years service in all, and described as 'one of the bravest men who lived'. No other lifeboatman has won as many medals. Five times he was awarded the Gold Medal and four times the Silver Medal. Other decorations included the George Cross and British Empire Medal. During his years, the Cromer boat went out 387 times and saved 873 lives.

Blogg was a modest man; and Cromer carries a modest air as other places strive to keep up to date. The feeling is that it will last the course better for 'keeping it simple'.

East Dereham

'Jolly Dereham… it is as near the centre of Norfolk as you can get. It lies just far enough from Norwich and Lynn to have its own ideas and its own discussions too.'
R.H. Mottram (1883-1971) *East Anglia*, 1933

Too much traffic and development sprawl put Dereham in serious danger of suffering cardiac arrest at the very heart of Norfolk. And yet the pulse of history beats proudly at every turn.

Spanning the High Street is the town sign illustrating the legend that St Withburga founded a nunnery here and was sustained during a famine by the milk of two deer. She has a well named after her to the west of the parish church. St Nicholas' was once at the centre of the town, which moved further west after a disastrous fire in 1581. Bishop Bonner's Cottages close to the church were among the few buildings to survive (*opposite*). Dated 1502, the thatched row is decorated by plaster pargeting and is now an impressive museum.

Edmund Bonner was Rector of Dereham from 1534 until 1540. He later became Bishop of London and gained notoriety for burning about 200 people at the stake during the heresy trial in Mary Tudor's reign.

There's a memorial window in St Nicholas' church to the poet William Cowper, who died in the town in 1800. South of Dereham is the small hamlet of Dumpling Green, where writer George Borrow was born in 1803.

Five miles north of Dereham, the attractive village of North Elmham (*inset*) was the seat of a Saxon bishop from AD 631 to 1071, before the bishopric moved first to Thetford and then to Norwich. The bishops continued to use North Elmham as a country retreat, and in the 14th century a fortified house was built here. The upper part of the ruins seen today are remains of that building. There are fine views over the countryside from this historic spot, which is open throughout the year.

Farmer's Glory

'Norfolk is a farming county. There one talks farming, thinks farming, dreams farming and lives farming… but the only farming which is considered worthy of notice is the type of farming which has been carried out in Norfolk since time immemorial.'

A.G. Street (1892-1966) *Country Calendar*, 1935

Mechanisation has transformed the efficiency of Norfolk farming, but has caused the disappearance of thousands of jobs. As a boy growing up in a small village in the middle of Norfolk just after the Second World War, I recall virtually every family being close to the land. Now such connections are exceptional.

For all that, farming remains the major industry, and, until recently, many other concerns were either supplying goods to the farming community – iron foundries, for example – or were based on farm products, such as mustard, brewing, malting and textiles.

Sugar beet is still regarded as the cornerstone crop with more than a third of the national acreage grown in the county and processed at factories at Wissington, near Downham Market, and Cantley, between Norwich and Yarmouth.

If 'Turnip' Townshend of the Raynham Estate and Coke of Holkham were the great innovators of the 18th and 19th centuries, Bernard Matthews of Witchingham Hall is the best known personality in Norfolk farming today. He started his empire in the 1950s with a few turkey eggs and built his company to be worth over £170 million and changed the nation's eating habits by making turkey a year-round non-luxury item. His national advertising campaign made 'bootiful!' the most famous of Norfolk words – although some of us much prefer the 'bewtiful' spelling.

A proud farming history is on display at the Norfolk Rural Life Museum at Gressenhall, near East Dereham, while many of the traditional practices and rare breeds are still flourishing on Union Farm just over the road. The museum garden (*inset*) features a wide variety of flowers, fruit and vegetables known to have been grown in Norfolk before 1920.

Due tribute is paid in the converted workhouse buildings to George Edwards, a key figure behind the formation of the National Union of Agricultural Workers. He started work at five years old as a crow scarer.

Sporting Colours

'A filly escaped from the course at Yarmouth and galloped along the seafront towards Caister. Her trainer Gerry Blum stopped a taxi and with the immortal words "Follow that horse!" tanked along the seafront after her. Two youngsters eventually stopped her and held her, to the trainer's relief.'

Richard Watts, *Norfolk Century*, 1999

While Norfolk may not be in the super league when it comes to sporting feats and facilities, there is much to engage participants and spectators alike – with Carrow Road the main theatre of dreams.

Home to Norwich City Football Club, the Canaries, it has staged many epic clashes over the seasons, including adventures against European giants Bayern Munich and Inter Milan in the early 1990s. The Canaries celebrated their centenary in 2001, narrowly missing a return to the Premiership after losing a penalty shoot-out in their promotion play-off with Birmingham.

Horse racing at Yarmouth and Fakenham (*opposite*) attracts loyal followers, both courses testament to the survival spirit and still at full gallop despite the presence nearby of pedigree-packed Newmarket. Norfolk does have two superb studs, the Royal Stud at Sandringham and the impressive set-up at Shadwell, just outside Thetford.

While Norfolk has to be content with minor counties status on the cricket scene, several outstanding home-grown products have moved on to the first-class and Test arenas, most notably Bill Edrich, John Edrich and Peter Parfitt. Cricket on the green in villages like Bradenham (*inset*) continues to nurture ambitions as well as keeping intact the game's traditional image.

Snetterton has been the home of Norfolk motor-sport since the Second World War. Speedway used to flourish in both Norwich and Yarmouth; now it revs up at King's Lynn. With so much water about, it's not surprising that sailing enjoys widespread support. It is hardly the privileged preserve of a century ago – while golf courses continue to multiply at the drop of a shot.

How's this for a proud punchline ... Jem Mace, the father of scientific boxing, was born in my home village of Beeston, near East Dereham, in 1831. The British and World champion has a memorial in the village churchyard.

Weybourne and Sheringham Park

'Some enchantment lies upon the coast of North Norfolk which leaves in memory, not just an impression of peculiar beauty, but a series of pictures standing out as vividly as if you had opened a book.'
Lilias Rider Haggard (1893-1968), *A Norfolk Notebook*, 1946

For many enthusiasts, locals and visitors alike, the first glimpse of Weybourne Mill (*opposite*) spells the beginning of 'real' coastline magic along the road from Sheringham to Hunstanton.

Privately owned and splendidly restored, this five-storey tower mill complete with cap and sails may not have been the subject of as many photographs and paintings as its close neighbour at Cley, but it casts a protective eye over a small but intriguing settlement packed with history and fresh interest since it was revealed that former Prime Minister John Major was buying a home here.

Weybourne (pronounced 'Webbun' by locals) has picturesque priory ruins next door to the parish church. The shingle beach, known as Weybourne Hope, shelves so steeply that deep draught boats can come within yards of the shore. Fears of invasion led to the establishment of an army camp before the last war. This is now a museum, the Muckleburgh Collection, featuring the biggest private collection in Britain of military equipment from battlefields all over the world.

For all Weybourne's attractions, it is well worth making a diversion on the other side of the road to take in the delightfully flint-built village of Upper Sheringham and the cultivated marvels of Sheringham Park (*inset*). Designed by Humphry Repton in the early 19th century, it fully deserves the accolade of 'Europe's Himalayas'.

The park is best visited in May and June when rhododendrons and azaleas are in full bloom.

A series of paths and wooden boardwalks suitable for wheelchairs allow visitors to see them at best advantage, while views from seated areas across the fields and woods to the sea are among the most prized in Norfolk. No wonder Repton considered this his finest work. Managed by the National Trust, the park is open all year, dawn to dusk. My fear of heights keeps me well away from the gazebo – although family and friends assure me the views are breathtaking!

Blakeney

'In the distance she could see the Point on the other side of the estuary, curving in like a great bent forefinger, enclosing an area of channels and sandbanks and shoals that, on a rising tide, was probably as lethal as anywhere on the Norfolk coast.'

Jack Higgins, *The Eagle Has Landed*, 1975

A three-mile long spit of storm-flung sand and shingle, Blakeney Point is internationally famous for its breeding colony of common seals and nesting terns. A wild and romantic spot with murky, open skies above, it is one of the oldest nature reserves in Britain, having been managed by the National Trust since 1912. Before that it was a favourite haunt of Victorian bird collectors.

Ted Eales, who took over from his father as warden in 1939, told me how the Point is always on the move and always changing: 'Not only the shape, but its moods as well. On a clear summer day, the sand is hot and white and the sea the pattern and colour of a tropical lagoon. Almost in an hour it can change to the harshness of the arctic scene, the sea grey and buckled and the sand driving the beaches in long twisted skeins.'

Thousands of visitors head for the Point each summer in boats leaving Morston and Blakeney Quay. There are excellent views of nesting terns, oystercatchers and ringed plovers from hides which should be approached by marked routes and boardwalks. Common seals, and the odd grey seal, can be seen throughout the year.

Blakeney itself (*inset*) is a most pleasing place with narrow lanes and flint cottages tumbling down to the harbour wall, hotels and shops. A fine church with two towers and a medieval guildhall are among other attractions. Yachts and pleasure craft crowd the small port in summer. At low tide there's a wide expanse of mudflats with the river trickling through, but at high tide boats can sail into the harbour.

Binham and Walsingham

*'At the time of the Dissolution, there were only six monks in residence ... Perhaps Walsingham,
so near, and so very much more attractive to rich pilgrims, caused the decay at Binham.'*
Doreen Wallace (1897-1989), *Norfolk*, 1951

It is easy to conjure up the formidable frame of Henry VIII and his impact on the county as you regard the glorious ruins of Binham Priory (*opposite*) and the bustling pilgrimage scene at Walsingham.

Founded in the late 11th century by Pierre de Valoines, nephew of William the Conqueror, Binham Priory surrendered to Henry's dissolution of the monasteries in 1540. Edward Paston, of the famous local family, intended to use the masonry to build a new manor house, but a worker was killed during demolition – and to this bad omen we owe the survival of the extensive ruins. The nave of the church continued in use as the parish church.

Today, the Priory Church of St Mary and the Holy Cross, to some extent a ruin within a greater ruin, is an inspiring and unique place of worship, especially in summer when services are held at the open-air altar.

Walsingham (*inset*), called 'England's Nazareth', was built on an 11th-century vision which fired the medieval mind and still continues to draw hundreds of thousands of visitors each year. Early in his reign, Henry VIII walked barefoot from Barsham nearby to place a gold necklace around the neck of the medieval statue of the Virgin. This did not, however, prevent him from suppressing the priory in 1538, when the statue was burned and most of the buildings demolished.

The renaissance of Walsingham as a shrine began with the first annual pilgrimage to the Roman Catholic Slipper Chapel in 1897. In 1921, the Rev Hope Patten was appointed Vicar at Walsingham and organised the first Anglican pilgrimage. The new Anglican shrine was opened and was greatly extended in 1937 to cope with the volume of visitors.

Heydon

*'Lodged deep in most of us is a need for roots and permanence, and the village symbolises
a place from which strength and reassurance may be drawn, where the past is always
present, neighbourliness is a way of life and where no man needs to be a stranger.'*

Richard Muir, *The English Village*, 1980

Any poll to find the most attractive village in Norfolk would inspire plenty of support for Heydon, glorying in its rural isolation amidst woods and farmland four miles west of Aylsham.

'A little paradise gathered about a green', waxed Arthur Mee when in the 1940s he dropped in on the Norfolk leg of his national tour for the 'King's England' series of books. Happily, that charm endures. Heydon remains a magnet for film makers and television producers. Cottages clustered around the green and the impressive parish church lend it an appealing bygone flavour. Heydon Hall presides paternally over this idyllic scene.

The handsome ornamental well on the green, a structure of red brick with terracotta dressings, was erected by Col W.E.G. Lytton Bulwer in 1877 to mark Queen Victoria's Golden Jubilee. Heydon Hall went up in the reign of Elizabeth I in 1584. In the park is a tree called Cromwell's Oak, named by Erasmus Earle, MP for Norwich in the Long Parliament. Earle lies under an altar tomb in the village church. The top of it is a stone 12 ft long and half as wide. Local legend claims it broke down three bridges on its journey and broke the back of one of the men who set it in position.

Inevitable past winner of Norfolk's Best Kept Village competition, Heydon is a place you can enter but not pass through. At the end of a cul-de-sac leading to the Hall, it is a lingering whiff of feudalism worth savouring. A blacksmith's forge (*inset*) faces rows of neat houses, some with pediments, some with step gables, and all with pretty front gardens. It looks and feels like the old Norfolk.

Wells-next-the-Sea

'By a lonesome road, here and there affording glimpses of distant ooze flats and sea creeks, growing chill and grey as the daylight wanes, I find my way into Wells, which I reach just in time to mingle with the latest loiterers on its quaint old quay.'

William A. Dutt, *Highways and Byways in East Anglia*, 1901

Despite increasingly seductive siren voices of the holiday trade, Wells clings to its nautical soul as befits the only port on the North Norfolk coast with a harbour suitable for commercial shipping. It has been a fishing centre and working port since at least the 13th century, and even today there are more whelks landed at Wells than at any other port in England.

Backcloth to all the quayside bustle is a vast flat expanse of saltmarsh, stretching like a patterned carpet to the horizon. The sea wall, which runs from the quay to Wells beach, is an excellent vantage point for bird watching – as well as one of the most popular perches for those who like to take a spot of fresh air with their fish and chips.

The sea wall was built by the Earl of Leicester in 1859, enabling land behind to be reclaimed for agriculture. Pines which back Wells beach were planted at about the same time to prevent wind-blown sand encroaching on this valuable new farmland.

South from the quay, a series of narrow lanes run up to the centre of town. Finest of these, Staithe Street (*inset*) has many attractive Victorian and Edwardian shop fronts. The southern end of the town has a different character again; a broad rectangular green called the Buttlands, because it was once used for archery practice, is lined with grand late-Georgian and Victorian houses.

The nearby parish church of St Nicholas, patron saint of sailors, was rebuilt after a fire in 1879. Buried in the churchyard is John Fryer, born in Wells in 1754. He was Master of the *Bounty*, the ship at the heart of the most famous mutiny in our maritime history.

Castle Acre

'... Castle Acre estate was bought ... by Coke of Norfolk in the 18th century. There is a tale which says that Coke owned so much land the King said he must not buy any more. But when Coke asked if he might buy one more acre, the request was granted. He bought Castle Acre – some 3,000 acres!'

Bernard Dorman, *Norfolk*, 1972

I have heard Castle Acre described as 'one of the best open-air history classrooms in the country'. Hard to argue with that if you want to touch the past in a village where little disturbs a strong sense of locality.

It is sited on the Peddars Way, the Roman trackway to the North Norfolk coast, and a day is scarcely long enough to take in the ancient beauties and importance of one of our finest examples of a Norman settlement.

William de Warenne's castle ruins (*opposite*) clasp the northern end of the village like giant arms and command wonderful views over the surrounding countryside. Founded just after the Norman Conquest, the castle received a number of kings of England over the centuries, including Henry III and Edward I. To the south-east of the village lie the glorious remains of a priory, the best-preserved Clunaic monastery in the country.

Although a village now, Castle Acre itself was once a fortified town, protected by its own bank, ditches and gateways. The southern and western parts of the town bank largely remain, while the so-called Bailey Gate was once the north gateway to the town. The medieval parish church shows it had outgrown its original boundaries by the 13th century. Cottages cluster now round the foot of the castle and up the steep narrow street leading to Stocks Green, a broad manicured lawn surrounded by smaller rural versions of Georgian town houses (*inset*).

The other two Acres, South and West, are worth visiting, albeit along narrow lanes, some so little used that grass grows in the middle.

Swaffham

'For those who care to think about it, Swaffham has always been a puzzle. A puzzle as to how and why it came to be an established and well-favoured place to live, especially when its position was not of the kind that led to the growth of most towns.'

Gerry Waldron, *Swaffham, The Making of a Town,* 2001

Often hailed as the finest predominantly Regency town in East Anglia, Swaffham still exudes a waft of elegance born out of times when posh county families moved in for 'the season'.

The market square is crowded with colourful stalls on Saturdays, drawing folk from a wide area to hunt for bargain bygones or to buy local produce. Focal point of the market place is the pillared Butter Cross – not a cross at all, but a circular pavilion built by Lord Orford in 1783 and crowned by a figure of Ceres, goddess of agriculture.

The privilege of holding a market at Swaffham was granted during King John's reign in about 1214. Until relatively recently the rights to hold the market and fairs were held solely by the Lord of the Manor of Swaffham, but now the town council administers the whole market, the biggest Saturday market in the region.

The sign standing proudly at the entrance depicts the story of John Chapman, the pedlar reputed to have found great treasure as a result of a dream. The sign was carved in 1929 by local craftsman Harry Carter. His cousin, Howard Carter, who uncovered the tomb of the Egyptian boy-king Tutankhamun, grew up here and has been dubbed 'the second Pedlar of Swaffham' since he discovered even greater treasure.

Carter Close, a collection of houses on the town's southern fringes, seems a rather unspectacular memorial to the man responsible for one of the most sensational archaeological finds of all time.

John Chapman's family pew (*inset*) is on the right-hand side of the chancel in the much-admired church of St Peter and St Paul. Legend has it that the Pedlar of Swaffham built the north side of the church in thanksgiving for finding treasure in his garden.

52

Thetford

'When erst in youth's gay prime and uncontrolled
O Thetford! round the flow'ry fields I've strolled,
From Tutt-Hill's eminence and Croxton's height,
Have viewed those ancient ruins with delight'
George Bloomfield, *Thetford Chalybeate-Spa,* 1821

The transformation of Thetford from sleepy country town into bustling industrial centre continues to spark passionate debates as to the merits of welcoming overspill population from London a decade or so after the Second World War.

Happily, a fair amount of old Thetford remains. There's a castle mound and a priory, numerous ancient buildings of local chalk block and flint and attractive open spaces by the river.

New estates and factories were beginning to mushroom when I arrived here in 1962 to start my career in local newspapers. I like to mention that another scribe, and one of note, began his scribbling days in Thetford ... Thomas Paine, the most remarkable political writer and radical thinker of the late 18th century, was born in Thetford in 1737, son of a maker of women's corsets. He produced a series of influential books and pamphlets advocating political and social change which championed the rights of the common man.

Paine played a prominent part in both the American and French Revolutions, but for many years after his death in 1809 he was disowned by his native town. It was only in 1964 that he was honoured by the erection of a gilded statue outside King's House (*opposite*), paid for by the Thomas Paine Foundation of America.

One of Thetford's most outstanding buildings, the Ancient House (*inset*), was a 15th-century merchant's house with magnificent carved timbers. It was bought in 1921 by Prince Frederick Duleep Singh and given to the town for use as a museum. The Prince's love for the town was underlined in his bequest of 90 portraits of East Anglian worthies.

Thetford Forest

'New beauties are perceptible with each succeeding dawn – a tinge of green here, a richer purple there, sun and cloud weaving the warp and woof of the panorama of colour in the landscape, flashing on the silver trunk of a birch or the ruddy richness of a Scots pine or plunging the distant woodland into a haze of blue.'

W.G. Clarke (1877-1925), *In Breckland Wilds,* 1923

The largest lowland forest in Britain, covering an area of 80 square miles, has a certain grandeur despite the uniformity it imposes on Breckland. Regiments of Corsican pine dominate, but the planting of broad-leaved trees has added welcome variety.

Wildlife abounds, with Norfolk's population of red squirrels leading the way. As part of a Species Recovery Programme, these are being bred in captivity and later released into the forest. Survival and behaviour are monitored by radio tracking and field observations. Strange to recall that in the 18th century red squirrels were so prolific that tens of thousands were killed as pests.

They do not damage trees, but the grey squirrel, so abundant since the 1960s, does serious harm to young plantings. In some parts of the forest, newly-planted areas may need protection from rabbits by fencing. Fallow, roe deer and muntjac and more than 70 different bird species make the forest their home; even the stone curlew, so typical of Breckland, is returning.

There are a number of way-marked walks and picnic places, although it should be noted that some parts of the forest are within the Ministry of Defence Battle Area and not accessible to the public.

Before the First World War much of Breckland was open heathland interspersed with arable farmland and woodland. There was no tradition of managing woods for timber production. Wartime shortages and awareness that most of the suitable trees had been felled gave rise to concern for the future and demonstrated the need to formulate a forestry policy. The Forestry Commission was set up and in 1922 a start was made on establishing Thetford Forest.

Oxburgh Hall

'From whatever angle it is viewed, Oxburgh makes so satisfying a composition in its setting and is so uniform in style that it continually suggests comparisons with painting, but for the park it is more like a fleeting manifestation of the spirit of the past.'

Olive Cook, *Breckland,* 1956

A war-like muster of gatehouse, towers and battlements reflected in a moat satisfy any immediate thoughts of medieval marauders being kept at bay. But an altogether more mellow mood takes hold as you savour the beauties of the Bedingfield family home.

Oxburgh Hall, on parade five miles south-west of Swaffham, was built by the Bedingfields in 1482, though the house of rose-coloured brick was given to the National Trust in 1952.

Visitors gasp in admiration at handiwork in the tapestry room. Displayed flat under glass in a controlled light to preserve them and show them to best advantage, these intricate embroideries were made in the 1500s by Mary, Queen of Scots and Elizabeth, Countess of Shrewsbury, two of the finest needlewomen of their day.

The magnificent Tudor gatehouse, an imposing example of early English brickwork, rises 80 ft from the moat and house. The roof of the tower offers a good view of the restored gardens, and on a clear day Ely Cathedral can be seen on the western horizon. The church of St John the Evangelist, just outside the grounds of the Hall, is partly in ruins following the collapse of the spire in 1948.

More history comes alive a couple of miles away with a unique reproduction of an Iceni settlement of the first century AD in the small village of Cockley Cley (*inset*).

Believed to be on the original site of a village dating from the time of Boadicea (Boudicca) – the fiery Iceni queen who led a revolt against the Romans – it nestles in a picturesque valley and attracts thousands of visitors each year.

Downham Market

*'Downham was noted for the sale of butter, fish and fowl. In the mid-18th century,
during spring and summer, about 3000 firkins of butter were regularly sold to factors,
who sent them by water to Cambridge and thence overland to London.'*

David Dymond, *The Norfolk Landscape,* 1985

Hard to believe it now as the town sits quietly on the edge of the Fens, but Downham Market was once a thriving inland port. The railway and a new canal cut it off from the river. There's been a settlement here since Roman times.

Much of the town is built of carrstone from local quarries, and this led to Downham being referred to at one time as the Gingerbread Town. There are several notable old buildings, some showing Dutch influence, with the market place dominated by the Gothic-style clock, Big Ben in miniature, an unusual cast–iron structure given to the town by James Scott in 1878 (*inset*).

After his defeat at Naseby, King Charles I visited Downham on May Day 1646. He was disguised as a clergyman and on his way to surrender to the Scottish army at Newark. He stayed overnight at an inn where the present Swan Hotel stands. George Manby, whose many inventions included the rocket life-saving apparatus, spent part of his schooldays in Downham.

Denver, a couple of miles from Downham, continues to play a significant role in the life of the area and beyond. Dutch engineer Vermuyden built the first sluice here in 1651 as part of a scheme to drain the fenlands. The oldest surviving sluice was built in 1834 and is still in use, though original wooden gates have been replaced with steel doors. Alongside is the new Great Denver Sluice

(*opposite*), opened in 1964. Together they perform several vital functions, controlling the flow of the rivers and, where necessary, diverting floodwaters into the flood relief channel that runs parallel to the Great Ouse.

The Fens

'What gives the Fens their particular character is not just the flatness, the space and light which are spoken of so frequently. Equally important are the shadows, mists, floods and blackness of winter. I have met fenmen who are pleased to see a misty day because it diminishes the vastness of the space around them.'

Edward Storey, *The Winter Fens,* 1993

Expanse and the majestic archway of overwhelming sky are main supports behind the gentle beauty of Fenland. There's fresh air to spare and wherever you travel, dykes, rivers and drains are constant companions.

Rivers and cuts are familiar and necessary features of low-lying areas. Norfolk's Marshland Fens occupy an area south and west of King's Lynn. This marshland is a result of pervading sea and fresh water flooding, and was once rich pastureland ideal for sheep rearing.

Many feel the pulse of Fenland history beating loudest at Welney (*inset*). The Old Bedford River reaches towards infinity in both directions. Isolated cottages along the bank, willow trees washing their feet in floodwater, scattered farms beyond ... and the smell of antiquity, dampness, richness and fertility.

Welney Wildfowl Centre is situated on the east end of the Ouse Washes, one of Europe's most important wintering grounds for wildfowl. Swans, widgeon, pochard and pintail duck are there in their thousands, and floodlighting at night enables visitors to see birds roosting around the lagoon. When the waters recede in spring, this refuge provides safe nesting sites for such birds as black tern, ruff and black-tailed godwit. There are hides, an excellent observatory, information displays and, in summer only, a nature trail.

Fenland is rich in fine churches, with the 'Queen of Marshland', Walpole St Peter, leading the way. It is perplexing that such magnificent buildings were sited in an area affording many difficulties to those who built them. And where did the money come from? The rich land gradually wrested from the sea must have passed untold wealth into farmers' hands as well as into the coffers of nearby friaries.

King's Lynn

'You can see the past effect of ownerships and individuality in Lynn as clearly as you can catch affection or menace in a human voice. The outward expression is most manifest, and to pass in and out along the lines in front of the old houses inspires in one precisely those emotions which are aroused by the human crowd.'
Hilaire Belloc (1870-1953), *The Hills and the Sea, 1906*

Despite over-hasty demolition and redevelopment after the Second World War, King's Lynn hangs on proudly to its historic core. A collection of medieval merchants' houses and warehouses probably not surpassed anywhere in the country maintains a reputation for conservation ahead of wholesale destruction.

In the 1950s, the docks were in decline and the population waning. Successful efforts were made to bring in new industry and an overspill scheme was negotiated with the London County Council. Then the docks revived as new housing estates and factories ringed the old town.

It took a while for Lynn to recover its poise standing on the Great Ouse on the shores of The Wash. From the 13th century, the Hanseatic League countries were Lynn's main trading partners, and Baltic ships are still frequent callers.

Lynn's main features are best seen on foot, with the Saturday Market Place an ideal starting-point near the beautiful St Margaret's church. Trinity Guildhall is opposite with its amazing chequered stone front.

The Custom House, built in 1683, has a statue to Charles I over the doorway, a reminder that Lynn supported the royal cause in the Civil War.

The father of one of the town's heroes, George Vancouver, was a customs officer here. A recently-unveiled bronze statue of the boy George stands before the Custom House (*inset*). He sailed with Captain Cook and is now rated among the most select band of explorer-navigators.

Red Mount Chapel, standing in a public park called The Walks, was built around 1485 beside the ancient pilgrims' way to Walsingham. This tiny octagonal building is noted for its fan-vaulted roof.

Castle Rising

'Rising was a seaport town
When Lynn was but a marsh,
Now Lynn it is a seaport
And Rising fares the worse.'
Traditional

This picture-postcard village's former importance is underlined by that verse. It was also a rotten borough, regularly returning two MPs to Parliament from 1558 to 1832. Sir Robert Walpole of Houghton Hall, our first Prime Minister, was among them. Now Castle Rising

lives in a world of its own off the busy King's Lynn to Sandringham road, knee-deep in history and compliments for the way it is looked after. A splendid medieval cross on a flight of steps stands on the small green which was once a market place. The Norman church peers down on Jacobean almshouses.

The Hospital of the Holy and Undivided Trinity is almost exactly as it was when Henry Howard, Earl of Northampton, ancestor of the present squire, built it in 1614 as an almshouse for 20 spinsters. It is a low brick building with little towers round a quadrangle with lawns and flowers round each old lady's door. Residents go to church in long red cloaks bearing the Howard badge and pointed black hats as they have done since the foundation.

Charm is at every turn, and to crown it all is the ruined castle (*inset*) with its row of firs providing a romantic aspect. Queen Isabella, Edward III's mother, was locked up here in 1330 following banishment for aiding her lover Roger Mortimer in the murder of Edward II. Although screams of Isabella's ghost are said to haunt the castle, her time in Castle Rising seems to have been spent in relative comfort.

With its fine domestic keep set in the centre of massive defensive earthworks, the site is open to the public and managed by English Heritage.

Sandringham

'When my grandfather preached here, he would stay at Sandringham House and once, at Christmas, organised the Royal Family for a sing-song round a piano with the Prince of Wales strumming a banjo and Queen Mary blowing through a comb wrapped in tissue paper.'

Tom Pocock, *Norfolk*, 1995

Sandringham House has been the Norfolk home of four generations of monarchs, and was first opened to the public in 1977. All main rooms occupied by the Royal Family when the Court is in residence are open during the summer months.

The 7,000 acre Sandringham Estate and its surrounding country park provide ideal habitat for the raising of game birds – wherein lay the attraction for the Prince of Wales, the future King Edward VII, whose New Year shooting parties established a tradition still followed today. The estate was bought for him for his coming of age in 1861 at a cost of about £220,000.

The original Georgian house was pulled down and replaced by a new building in Jacobean style, to which a lavish turreted ballroom and room for bowls and billiards were later attached.

George VI had the lovely north garden laid out with box hedges and pleached lime alleys, interplanted with lavender and roses. In spring and summer a succession of rhododendrons and azaleas show off their colourful blooms, while lakes excavated in the 19th century are fringed with irises, arum lilies and giant gunneras.

Outside the gardens, numerous nature trails thread through Sandringham Country Park, best visited in early summer when naturalised rhododendrons fill the woods with colour.

The carrstone church of St Mary Magdalene on the estate (*inset*), much restored by the Victorians, has become embedded in the British tradition. The Royal Family attend services here at Christmas, watched by large crowds. By this time the Queen has already recorded her Christmas message. Her father and grandfather sat before the microphone in the library at Sandringham House to address their Empire.

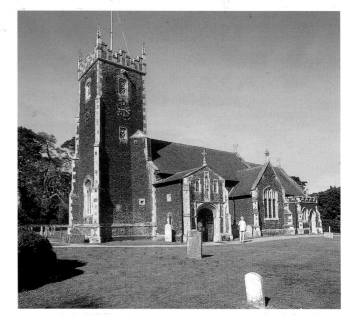

Hunstanton

'The most curious thing about this place is the celebrated cliff, so full of interest to the geologist. Here it is that the Prince and Princess of Wales are in the habit of taking luncheon, a servant laying the cloth on one of the rocks, while the future King of England sits on another, smoking his cigar.'

The Rev Benjamin Armstrong (1817-1890), *Norfolk Diary*, 1864

Ranging in colour from gingerbread to white, those striped cliffs towering over sweeping sands and shallow waters give Hunstanton a timeless tint on a fast-changing seaside scene. It has the unique distinction of being the only resort on the east coast to face west. It takes newcomers some time to get used to the apparent phenomenon of seeing the sun set over the sea instead of the land.

Around 1840 there was nothing between Old Hunstanton and Heacham. Henry Styleman Le Strange, Lord of the Manor and hereditary Lord High Admiral of the Wash, decided to develop the area south of the old village as a sea bathing resort. The town was described as 'the poor man's St Moritz'.

The coming of the railway in 1862 helped make New Hunstanton fashionable for genteel holidays. It survived the original Beeching cuts but was closed in 1969. Hunstanton Pier, built in 1870, was destroyed in a heavy storm on the night of 11th January 1978. In Hunstanton's Esplanade Gardens there is a memorial plaque bearing the names of 31 people who lost their lives in the 1953 East Coast floods, 15 of them British and the other 16 citizens of the United States. An American named Reis Leming saved 27 lives and was awarded the George Medal.

Known as 'Hunstan' by true locals, and dubbed 'Sunny Hunny' by ever-optimistic tourist officials, the place has enchanted writers over the years. Novelist L. P. Hartley (1895-1972) turned Hunstanton into 'Anchorstone' in his Eustace and Hilda trilogy, while the resort was familiar territory for humourist and writer P. G. Wodehouse (1881-1975).

Old Hunstanton (*inset*), half a mile to the north, is mainly residential, nestling prettily behind the sand dunes.

The Lavender Fields

'The Women's Institute survey disclosed a variety of parish events … church fetes, fairs, sales of home produce, and – in the case of one woman who sits in the church porch selling bundles of lavender gathered from the churchyard of St Margaret's at Cley in Norfolk – churchyard produce.'
Francesca Greenoak, *Wildlife in the Churchyard*, 1985

Those on the scent of a good yarn in Norfolk invariably take in Heacham and its connections with Pocahontas, the Red Indian princess featured on the village sign and in a portrait in the parish church. She married local man John Rolfe in 1614 and became a celebrity in this country. Sadly, our climate did not agree with her and she died only three years later at the age of 22.

Heacham's current claim to fame, however, is as home to England's only lavender farm, at Caley Mill at the junction of the A149 and B1454. Lavender is harvested during July and early August and this is when tours can best be enjoyed. At other times of the year, the National Collection of Lavenders can be seen here, set in two acres of grounds. There is also a 19th-century water mill. The farm was founded in 1932 and now occupies over 100 acres. Five varieties of lavender are grown for distilling and a further two for drying.

Ringstead Downs nearby is one of the few chalk grasslands left in Norfolk. It is noted for rich plant life, while birds and butterflies flourish as well.

The Gin Trap Inn at Ringstead (*inset*) is a former 17th-century coaching inn tastefully renovated. Situated close to the Peddars Way, it is popular with walkers. Some of the old traps have been neatly converted to electric wall lights, while another decoration in the form of rural implements covers the ceiling. There's an original set of stocks in one of the car parks … so reasonable standards of behaviour are encouraged!

Brancaster

'She climbed the dunes, making her way along paths scratchy with marram grass and sea gorse … she made her way down to the sands. There, in the sharp morning light, each small stone and shell made its particular shadow. A single seagull kited above her, rising and falling, pulled by an invisible string.'
Angela Huth, *Invitation to the Married Life*, 1991

For many, the tranquillity and stability of life along the Norfolk coast is most vividly expressed in a walk on Brancaster beach ... preferably under wind-torn skies in winter. Novelist Angela Huth has described standing alone here one Christmas, 'looking at the great emptiness and thinking there is nowhere on earth more beautiful.'

Brancaster survives on tourism and shell-fishing. Mussels are farmed in the harbour, transplanted here from spawning grounds in The Wash, and whelks are dredged from the sea bed. Local boatmen also provide trips to Scolt Head Island, an important site for terns, oystercatchers and ringed plovers and capable of being a wild and lonely spot.

Just under four miles long, the sand and shingle bank is changing shape continuously. It was originally bought from Lord Leicester of Holkham Hall in 1923. The Norfolk Naturalists' Trust purchased the eastern tip in 1945, and it is now managed by English Nature. A marked trail ensures minimum disturbance to birdlife on the island.

Access is by boat from Brancaster Staithe, and it is strongly advised that visitors should not try to walk out to the island at low tide. The salt marshes and salt flats can be very dangerous to those not wholly familiar with them.

The Royal West Norfolk Golf Club at Brancaster is a treeless links course dominated by the surrounding marshes and dunes.

Pretty cottages with roses round the door (*inset*) guard the beach in this place formerly called Branodunum as the Romans established their northernmost Norfolk fort. Its commander was given the accolade 'Count of the Saxon Shore'.

Ecclesiastical Gems

'Elwin was confident that, like Wren, he was building for eternity. To some extent luck was with him, for the combination – normally fatal – of hard cement and soft stone was protected by slate pegs and exceptionally thin joints.'
From the guide to Booton church, published by the Redundant Churches Fund.

A magnificent monument to Victorian enthusiasm rises out of the surrounding trees at little Booton, a mile east of Reepham. The Cathedral of the Fields (*opposite*), one of the most extraordinary churches in the country, was created by a gifted eccentric.

Rector of Booton for 50 years, Whitwell Elwin began rebuilding the village church in the 1870s, his remarkable design including details from as far afield as Venice and early churches in Egypt. He had no architectural training

and no ability as a draughtsman – but the pinnacles and towers still draw gasps of astonishment. Materials used were limestone from Bath and black knapped flints from the beach at Mundesley on the North Norfolk coast.

The Church of St Michael the Archangel, described by leading architect of the day, Edwin Lutyens, as 'very naughty, but built in the right spirit', was vested in the Redundant Churches Fund in 1987. Occasional services are still held.

From village angels to a heavenly host in town ... and the glorious double hammerbeam roof in the church of St Peter and St Paul at Swaffham (*inset*). This chestnut-wood construction was designed to bridge a wide span with a minimum of outward thrust, so it is efficient as well as beautiful.

Carved angels with outstretched wings, 88 in all, decorate the end of the hammerbeams and either side of the king posts above collar beams. A further 104 angel carvings are set along the wall plate on either side. All bear shields showing the insignia and instruments of The Passion.

When the roof was restored late in the 19th century, small bullets or slugs were found embedded in the angels. Some think they had been fired by Cromwell's men in an effort to destroy out-of-reach images. Others feel they were fired to drive away nesting birds.

Grimes Graves

'Those flints that on the warren lie
And glint in moonlight like a snake's eye,
Though chipped by knappers for flint arrows
That flew away like sparrows,
Are still so fresh that one might say
Those dead men were on holiday.'
Andrew Young, *At Grimes Graves*, 1960

It looks more like a lunar landscape or war-time bombing range. It sounds like an ancient burial ground on a desolate stretch of heathland ...

Grimes Graves, however, is one of the oldest industrial sites in Europe, an extensive group of flint mines dating back to the late Neolithic period of about 4,000 years ago. The site is dotted with grass-covered hollows, 366 of which can be seen on the surface. Excavations have shown that beneath these hollows are shafts, now completely infilled, cut through sand, boulder and chalk.

From the bottom of each shaft radiated a number of galleries in which miners, using antler picks, extracted high-quality flint. One of the mines is open to the public. Although for safety reasons visitors are not allowed to crawl along the tunnels, it is possible to climb right down the shaft and see its seven galleries. An excellent display area in the custodian's hut describes the history of Grimes Graves, and the custodian is usually on hand to give a demonstration of the ancient art of flint knapping – the clever and calculated use of a flint hammerstone to knock off flakes from a large lump of flint.

The name Grimes Graves was probably given to it by the Saxons, who thought the area of grassy hollows was created by Grim (Woden), chief of the Anglo-Saxon gods. This fascinating site is in the care of English Heritage and open daily.

Weeting Castle nearby (*inset*) lies at the end of a deeply potholed track north of the village of Weeting. It consists of an aisled hall with cross wings and the remains of a three-storey tower, originally built around 1180. The castle is maintained also by English Heritage.

Norfolk with its beaches, old mills, inland waterways, salt marshes, castle ruins, lavender fields, restored railway and great houses is a county to explore and enjoy. Through the images of expert photographer, Robert Hallmann, and the commentary of well-known local author and broadcaster, Keith Skipper, this book celebrates the county in all its glory.

Robert Hallmann has lived in East Anglia for most of his life. His first major photographic exhibition was in London in 1978. Since then he has won a number of local and national competitions and was runner-up in a Kobal – *Independent on Sunday* Portrait Competition with an exhibition at the National Portrait Gallery. His illustrated books include *The Landscapes of Essex* and *Essex – Off the Beaten Track.*

Keith Skipper was born and brought up in Norfolk. He is the author of many books on his home county including *Hidden Norfolk* and *Hev Yew Gotta Loight, Boy?* a memoir of Norfolk's Singing Postman. In 1999 he helped to found FOND – Friends of Norfolk Dialect.

Front cover photograph: The Broads near Burgh Castle
Back cover photograph: Winterton-on-Sea